You Got The Jewels But I Got The Dagger

Davronia "Val" Scarbrough

Scripture quotations marked (ASV) are quoted from the American Standard Version, a work of public domain.

Scripture quotations marked (NIV) are taken from the Holy Bible, New International Version®, NIV®. Copyright © 1973, 1978, 1984, 2011 by Biblica, Inc.® Used by permission of Zondervan. All rights reserved worldwide. www.zondervan.com The "NIV" and "New International Version" are trademarks registered in the United States Patent and Trademark Office by Biblica, Inc.®

Scripture quotations marked (ERV) are taken from the Holy Bible: Easy-to-Read Version (ERV), International Edition © 2013, 2016 by Bible League International and used by permission.

Scripture quotations marked (NKJV) are taken from the New King James Version®. Copyright © 1982 by Thomas Nelson. Used by permission. All rights reserved.

You Got the Jewels, But I Got the Dagger

Copyright © 2025. All rights reserved— Davronia "Val" Scarbrough

No part of this book may be reproduced or transmitted in any form or by any means, graphic, electronic, or mechanical, including photocopying, recording, taping, or by information storage retrieval system without the written permission of the publisher. The contents and cover of this book may not be reproduced in whole or in part in any form without the express written permission of the author or publisher.

ISBN: **978-0-9995498-9-6**

Please direct all copyright inquiries to:
ScarbroughED
PO Box 803
Harrisburg, NC 28075

Acknowledgments

I always take time to thank The Father because when He chose me to come into the earth, He chose me for a reason. It is my pleasure to bring the portion of His dream to pass through me. Every word written, every lesson learned, and every experience shared is part of His divine plan, and for that, I am eternally grateful.

Thank You, Jesus, my Savior—for saving me, loving me, interceding for me, and being patient with me. Your sacrifice, your grace, and your unyielding love continue to sustain me daily.

Thank You, Holy Spirit, for leading me and guiding me into all truth. The promise in **John 16:13** lives daily in my life, and I am thankful for your voice, your wisdom, and your gentle yet firm direction.

To my husband, Eddie—thank you for always inspiring me to go for it, to never hold back, and to boldly walk in what God has called me to do. You are truly my biggest cheerleader. The Word says, "No greater love than this than a man who lays down his life for a friend" (John 15:13). I am grateful to be doing life with you—a perfect match made in heaven!

To my spiritual daughters—you have invited me into your life space, and I do not take that lightly. Thank you for trusting me to build you in the Word, to pour into you, and for allowing me to walk alongside you in your vulnerabilities, your struggles, your growth, your wins, and your ministry. It is an honor to call you daughters.

To my mother—thank you for introducing me to writing when I was only **sixteen**.

You directed me to a love that would become a lifelong passion, and I haven't put the pen down since.

Davronia Val Scarbrough

To our spiritual parents, Apostles Tony and Cynthia Brazelton—thank you for directing our purpose, for speaking into our lives, and for lovingly guiding us in the moments that mattered most. Your wisdom and covering have made all the difference.

To all the spiritual leaders who have been purposefully placed in our path—thank you for your wisdom, your guidance, and your deposits into our lives. I am grateful for every lesson, every correction, and every moment of encouragement that has shaped this journey.

To my natural daughters, my first spiritual children. The road has sometimes been bumpy, but through it all, thank you for trusting me with your **lives**. It is an honor to be your mother, and I pray you are proud of this work.

I trusted God as I dove into this subject—a subject that can be difficult, misunderstood, and even taboo—but I know it was necessary. I pray this book speaks life, healing, and wisdom to all who read it.

With love,
Val

Prologue

I knew it was time to release this book while ministering at a women's conference on relationships. As I spoke about the importance of godly connections, I felt a deep stirring in my spirit—this wasn't just about marriages or friendships. There was a greater conversation that needed to be had, one that often goes unspoken but carries deep wounds and lasting impact: the relationship between spiritual fathers and mothers and their sons and daughters.

*F*irst of all, I don't want this book to sound like a blame game scenario. That is not my heart. I want to be the first to admit that there were missteps on my part as a spiritual leader. I didn't always get it right. There were moments I could have handled better, words I could have spoken differently, and lessons I could have taught with more grace. But if there's one thing I've learned, it's that spiritual leadership is a journey—one that requires humility, constant learning, and an unwavering dependence on God.

*W*hen you step into the shoes of a spiritual parent, you quickly realize there is a thin line—no, I would say a hairline—that must always be considered. As you build a relationship with another child of God, you must acknowledge that two different backgrounds, experiences, and perspectives are coming together to become one in the faith. And that? That is a choreographed dance with so many intricate moves that you have to stay before God just to navigate the ebbs and flows of the relationship. One wrong step, one miscalculated move, and what was meant to be a beautiful partnership in the Spirit can become a source of pain for both parties.

Davronia Val Scarbrough

*L*et me be clear: it was never our intention to damage anyone. But we must acknowledge that there is an enemy out there whose sole objective is to blur intentions, distort truth, and create wounds where there should have been wisdom. The adversary's greatest weapon is deception, and if we are not careful, he can manipulate even the purest of hearts.

*F*leeting moments of listening to the wrong voice—of offense, pride, or misunderstanding—can place a dagger in the hands of the most beautiful people.

*A*nd before they even realize it, they've wounded someone they were meant to honor. Jesus warned Peter, "The devil desires to sift you like wheat" (Luke 22:31). Peter wasn't an evil man. He wasn't filled with malice. He was devoted to Jesus, yet in a weak moment, he denied the very One he loved. That is the nature of spiritual warfare—it doesn't always come in obvious attacks. Sometimes, it sneaks in through a whisper, a moment of pride, or an unchecked wound.

*T*his is why, according to the Word of God, everyone should have a teacher, a mentor, or a spiritual father/mother on their journey. We were never meant to navigate faith alone. The Bible shows us patterns of divine order—Moses had Joshua, Elijah had Elisha, Paul had Timothy. God establishes these relationships not to create hierarchy but to provide guidance, correction, and covering. However, when these relationships are misunderstood or mismanaged, they can become sources of great pain instead of great blessing. So, this book is not about casting blame. It is about healing.

*I*t is about helping both spiritual parents and spiritual sons and daughters understand the weight of these relationships and the enemy's strategy to divide and destroy them. My prayer is that as you read these pages, you will find wisdom, clarity, and, most of all, the grace to heal where healing is needed. Because in this hour, the body of Christ must get this relationship right.

There is too much at stake!

Pastor Val

Davronia Val Scarbrough

What Readers Are Saying...

This writing boldly answers the hard questions many shy away from—delivering truth wrapped in honesty, transparency, and pastoral wisdom. With a heart to bring clarity and correction to the Body of Christ, Pastor Val writes from a place of deep spiritual insight and conviction. Having personally studied spiritual fathers in ministry for several years, I can say this author has invested invaluable time, prayer, and discernment into exposing the misuse of spiritual authority, particularly where leadership has become more about power than purpose. One of the most impactful truths was the reminder that the office of authority is not a throne—it's an altar. In a culture where leaders sometimes serve from a place of ego and entitlement, this writing calls us to humility, servant leadership, and divine accountability. The writing doesn't just point out dysfunction—it shines light on what healthy spiritual authority should look like. The structure of the chapter I read was clear, the message is Spirit-led, and the call is urgent. Pastor Val has written with the precision of a teacher and the compassion of a true shepherd.

Pastor Gregg Morris, New Zion Missionary Baptist, Northport, AL

What Readers Are Saying…

Authentic, transparent, and biblically grounded—this book is a true reflection of Pastor Val's heart and calling. With profound wisdom drawn from both personal experience and the Word of God, she brings much-needed healing and clarity to the often-misunderstood relationship between spiritual parents and children. Pastor Val masterfully shares her journey with vulnerability and strength, weaving together powerful truths that offer correction, restoration, and deep insight. She doesn't shy away from the difficult topics but instead leans in with compassion and conviction, making space for real conversations and real growth. Whether you're walking as a spiritual parent or navigating life as a spiritual child, this book will meet you where you are. It will bless you, challenge you, and leave you better than before equipped with a greater understanding of honor, alignment, and the beauty of covenant relationships in the Kingdom of God.

Roshanda Pratt, Columbia, SC

This book was an easy yet powerful read, filled with sound wisdom and spiritual guidance that resonates deeply. The chapter I read was incredibly insightful, and I truly appreciated Pastor Val's candor and sincerity. Her heart for leadership and for those who serve under it is evident in every line. The bonus chapter on spiritual malfeasance stood out the most—it tackled the often-misunderstood topic of "church hurt" with grace, maturity, and compassion. I had never heard it explained in such a thoughtful way. The phrase was introduced with care, and what made it even more impactful was Pastor Val's willingness to take ownership and offer an apology for any past missteps—a rare and honorable gesture in leadership. The structure of the narrative was clear, heartfelt, and easy to follow, making the message both accessible and meaningful. This book is a refreshing and much-needed voice in the Body of Christ.

Minister Michelle Rouche, San Antonia, TX

Davronia Val Scarbrough

TABLE OF CONTENTS

PART 1 - The Dagger—The Heartbreak of Spiritual Parenthood

Chapter One	When the One You Poured Into Walks Away
Chapter Two	The Wounds of Misunderstanding
Chapter Three	The Cost Impartation

PART 2 - The Jewels - The Reward of Spiritual Fathering and Mothering

Chapter Four	They Called You Father/Mother Until You Corrected Them
Chapter Five	When Sons and Daughters Return with Wisdom
Chapter Six	Spiritual Legacy – What You Build Will Outlive You
Chapter Seven	True Sonship Is Proven, Not Just Claimed

PART 3 – Healing and Restoration

Chapter Eight	Loving Beyond Betrayal
Chapter Nine	How Precious are the Jewels to You?
Chapter Ten	The Joy of Spiritual Legacy – Flourishing Sons, Daughters and Heavenly Reward
Chapter Eleven	The Gift of Spiritual Motherhood – Lessons from Ruth and Naomi
Chapter Twelve	Ruth's Perspective: The Heart of a Spiritual Daughter
Bonus	Malfeasance

Ok, Let's Talk About It...

When we think about spiritual jewels, we must first ask, what are they? Why are they significant? The Bible often uses jewels as a symbol of value, wisdom, inheritance, and divine adornment. These jewels are not just physical riches, but spiritual gifts and treasures entrusted to us by the Father—faith, hope, wisdom, covering, and spiritual strategies that shape our destiny.

What Does the Bible Say About Jewels?

Throughout Scripture, jewels are used as symbols of God's favor, adornment, and spiritual wealth. In Isaiah 49:18, God speaks to His people: *"Lift up your eyes and look around; all your children gather and come to you. As surely as I live," declares the Lord, "you will wear them all as ornaments; you will put them on, like a bride."*

And in **Ezekiel 16:11-13**, God describes how He adorned Israel:

"I adorned you with jewelry: I put bracelets on your arms and a necklace around your neck, and I put a ring on your nose, earrings on your ears and a beautiful crown on your head. So, you were adorned with gold and silver; your clothes were of fine linen and costly fabric and embroidered cloth."

This isn't just about physical beauty—it's about God's divine covering, His investment in us, and the spiritual riches He bestows upon His people.

The Meaning of Different Jewels in the Bible
- **Diamonds** – Strength and endurance (Exodus 28:18)
- **Sapphires** – Divine favor and wisdom (Ezekiel 1:26)
- **Rubies** – Priceless worth and virtue (Proverbs 31:10)
- **Emeralds** – Life and growth (Revelation 21:19)
- **Gold** – Refinement, glory, and kingship (Malachi 3:3)

These jewels symbolize attributes of God and His gifts to His people—and just as physical jewels must be stewarded and protected, so must the spiritual jewels we receive.

The Purpose of Stewarding Spiritual Jewels

Faith, hope, wisdom, covering, and spiritual strategies—these are our spiritual jewels. They are not meant to be hoarded; they are meant to be stewarded, developed, and passed down.

We see this clearly in the story of Elisha and the widow woman in 2 Kings 4. She came to him in desperation, and instead of just giving her money, Elisha gave her a strategy. He asked her, *"What do you have in your house?"* and through his wisdom, she was able to multiply what she already had. This was a spiritual jewel of "strategy"—that changed her life forever.

The Sword

I have always found the medieval era fascinating, not all of it, but the sport "jousting" in particular. Jousting required skill, precision, and courage, but what I found most interesting was the craftsmanship of the swords and armor used by noble knights. A **jousting sword**, particularly the handle, was often adorned with jewels. The more intricate and decorative the handle, the higher the rank and significance of the knight. The jewels on the sword weren't just for display—they represented honor, victory, and divine favor. This parallels our spiritual walk—our jewels represent the victories, wisdom, and favor we carry in the kingdom. They are marks of divine honor, and how we steward them determines how we advance in the kingdom. Much like the nobleman's sword—elegant and adorned with jewels yet still crafted to wound its opponent—Jewels & Daggers often exist together. This is why stewarding the jewels is so significant in spiritual relationships, why, because you never want to "place your jewels in a dagger".

This is why nothing can go unchecked or unhealed in the relationship of Spiritual Parent/Spiritual Child, Mentor/Mentee or even in our natural relationships; why, because the very thing meant to bless can be used to wound deeply. Spiritual leadership and mentorship are about "stewardship". We don't just carry titles—we carry **jewels** that must be passed down to the next generation. This has to be our whole focus.

We must see faith, hope, wisdom, covering, and spiritual strategies as precious jewels—not to be wasted or used improperly, but to be used for the advancement of the kingdom.

So, the question remains: How will you steward the jewels given to you?

ENJOY THIS LABOR OF LOVE!

Stewardship: the careful and responsible management of something entrusted to one's care, encompassing resources, time, talents, and possessions, with a focus on ethical and sustainable practices.

Mentorship: the guidance provided by a mentor, especially an experienced person in a company or educational institution.

Covering: a thing used to cover something else, typically in order to protect or conceal it.

Spiritual Parenting: involves a collaborative relationship where an experienced guide (mentor) provides insight, wisdom, and support to help a mentee navigate their spiritual journey and deepen their connection with the divine.

You Got The Jewels But I Got The Dagger

Part One

Davronia Val Scarbrough

What Readers Are Saying...

This work is laced with the voice of healing and restoration for both parties involved. Whether you were the one who received the jewels or the dagger, the message is clear—there's still room to grow. What really stood out was how the chapter oozes with the love of Jesus Christ, offering grace, perspective, and wisdom.

Unlike other books on this subject, this one feel deeply personal yet powerfully universal, possibly surpassing similar works by the way it speaks to leaders and followers alike.

The author writes not from a place of victimhood, but from experience and victory, aiming to bring healing to the entire Body of Christ.

Pastor Eddie Scarbrough, Transforming Life Church Charlotte, NC

Chapter One

When the One You Poured into Walks Away

I know you may be wondering, Why I would start a book of this magnitude with such a tone? Couldn't you have walked us up to this moment? Of course I could have, that would seem like the right approach, but I think starting with the raw emotion of separation will help navigate this book to the end goal of healing. Because before we talk about restoration, we must acknowledge the pain. Before we discuss wisdom, we must deal with the wounds.

No matter how strong you are in faith, nothing fully prepares you for the pain of watching someone you've poured into walk away. It's a unique kind of heartbreak—one that spiritual fathers and mothers know all too well

If you've ever poured into someone—spiritually, emotionally, or even mentally—you know the deep bond that forms in the process. You don't just teach; you invest. You don't just guide; you love. And when that relationship is severed, whether through betrayal, offense, or simply a quiet departure, it cuts in a way that words struggle to express.

Jesus Himself experienced this. Judas wasn't just a follower; he was family. He sat at the table, walked the journey, and saw firsthand the power of Christ's love. And yet, when deception entered his heart, he made a devastating choice.

Davronia Val Scarbrough

One of the greatest heartbreaks a spiritual parent can face is when a son or daughter you've walked with, prayed over, and believed in turns away. Not just leaving the relationship, but sometimes, leaving you with the feeling of being wounded with a dagger. The one you once embraced may now speak against you. The one you once covered may now expose your faults. And the one you would have laid down your life for may now act as if you never mattered at all.

The Weight of Betrayal from Those You Loved

Jesus knew this pain well. Judas was not just a disciple; he was part of the inner circle. He walked with Jesus, witnessed the miracles, and broke bread at the same table. Yet, in a fleeting moment of deception, he turned away—not with honesty, not with closure, but with a dagger hidden in the form of a kiss.

What makes betrayal so painful is not just the act itself, but *who* it comes from. If it were an enemy, it would be expected. But when it's someone you considered family, it shakes you to your core. Psalm 55:12-14 ESV captures this heartbreak:

"For it is not an enemy who taunts me—then I could bear it; it is not a foe who rises against me—then I could hide from him. But it is you, a man like myself, my companion and close friend. We had sweet fellowship together; we walked with the crowd into the house of God."

Sound familiar? It should. If you've ever had a spiritual son or daughter walk away, you know this feeling all too well.

Jesus and Judas—When the Closest One Turns Against You

Jesus' response to Judas teaches us something profound. When Judas came to betray Him, Jesus still called him *friend* (Matthew 26:50).

Not sarcastically. Not in bitterness. But because Jesus understood something we often miss—betrayal does not change identity. The enemy may have deceived Judas, but Judas was still someone Jesus loved.

This is where it gets hard for us. When we are hurt, our natural response is to label people with their last offense. We call them *traitors* or *users*. We replay the hurt repeatedly until the pain consumes us. But Jesus shows us another way. He never ignored the betrayal, but He refused to let it define Him—or Judas.

The reality is, it doesn't take much—just a quick moment of entertaining the wrong voice: pride, offense, or even simple misunderstanding—and suddenly, someone you love, and trust is holding a dagger. Even the most well-meaning, beautiful people can be swayed by emotion or assumption, and before they even realize it, they've wounded someone they were actually called to walk with, cover, or honor. It rarely starts with bad intentions. Sometimes it's just hurt left unchecked, or questions left unanswered. But that one moment, if not brought into the light, can shift the entire course of a relationship.

These relationships—no matter how pure the intentions—are always subject to spiritual warfare, because the enemy knows the power of true alignment. When spiritual parents and children walk in unity, kingdoms are advanced and chains are broken, which is exactly why the enemy works overtime to plant offense, misunderstanding, and division. If Satan could deceive Judas, a man who sat at the feet of Jesus, then it should not surprise us that the enemy can cloud the hearts of those we pour into.

How to Keep Your Heart Pure When Wounded

So, what do you do when the one you pour into walks away? How do you keep your heart from turning cold?

1. **Acknowledge the Pain, but Don't Let It Consume You**
   - It's okay to grieve. It's okay to feel. Even Jesus was troubled in spirit when He spoke of Judas' betrayal (John 13:21). <u>But don't let pain become your permanent posture</u>.

2. **Refuse to Retaliate**
   - One of the greatest temptations is to defend yourself in ways that are not God-honoring. (I know this feeling all too well) But Jesus, even when accused and betrayed, did not lash out. He trusted God with His vindication.

3. **Pray for Them, Even When It Hurts**
   - This is the hardest step, but it is the most necessary. Prayer keeps bitterness from taking root. It keeps your spirit aligned with God, even when your heart is broken.

4. **Remember Who Called You**
   - Your assignment was never about a person—it was about God. If you focus on the pain, you'll miss the purpose. Keep moving forward. Keep leading. Keep loving.

Conclusion

Leadership is a sacred assignment. It's not just about titles, positions, or platforms, it's about stewardship, trust, and the responsibility to guide others well. If there's anything I want you to take from this chapter, it's this: leadership will cost you something. Pouring into people isn't always easy, and sometimes, the very ones you invest in will walk away. But that doesn't mean the investment was wasted. Every lesson, every impartation, every moment of covering still carries weight in the kingdom. When you've poured your heart into someone—given them your best, prayed for them, walked with them through their struggles, and then watched them leave—it can feel personal. But leadership isn't about holding on to people; it's about being faithful to the assignment, whether they stay or go.

<u>Journal Your Personal Prayer:</u>

What Readers Are Saying...

The word "no" is a powerful yet often polarizing term. For some, both giving and receiving it can be incredibly empowering, while for others, it can feel disheartening. These emotional responses can be heightened in the context of the church, where the use of "no" can have a profound impact on relationships, influencing trust and leading to either positive outcomes, such as strengthened boundaries and mutual respect, or negative consequences, such as misunderstandings and weakened bonds.

In this insightful chapter, Pastor Val skillfully explores not only the will of God but also the spiritual posture that both leaders and sons and daughters should adopt when navigating the complexities of the word "no." She further reveals the transformative benefits of "no" from both leadership and sonship perspectives. One of the key points that stood out for me was the importance of leaders clearly articulating their "no."

Through this clear and engaging read, Pastor Val leaves no question unanswered by strategically guiding readers through the deeper meaning and purpose of the word "no," and by highlighting how spiritual maturity and understanding can foster significant relational and personal growth when a "no" is given and received with the right heart.

This chapter is thoughtfully crafted with a clear and engaging narrative as Pastor Val offers an evolved biblical perspective on an age-old issue.

Christina Stoton, Empire Christian Center, Albany, NY

Chapter Two

The Wounds of Misunderstanding

Let's start with a simple question: What is a misunderstanding? A misunderstanding is a failure to understand something correctly—whether it involves words, intentions, or actions. In relationships, especially spiritual ones, misunderstandings can feel like small cracks that, if not addressed, can split the foundation wide open. They often come from unspoken expectations, assumptions, or differing perspectives and can cause offense where none was intended. So,

how do we handle different viewpoints in the Kingdom of God? How do we navigate the growing pains that come when a leader says "No", or "Wait", or the big one—"Have faith for it".

These words challenge our timing, our trust, and often our pride. But if we're willing to lean into the process instead of pulling away, we'll find that misunderstandings don't have to lead to

disconnection. It can actually lead to deeper understanding and stronger relationships when handled with grace, humility, and open communication.

I remember a moment in time when I had to say no to one of our spiritual daughters. She was eager to go and deliver a word at a particular place, fully convinced she was ready. But in my spirit, I just didn't have a release to say, yes, go ahead and preach the house down.

Now, let me pause here and be clear—this was not about control, manipulation, or dictatorship. The beauty of spiritual covering is that it provides wisdom, guidance, and protection from a place of experience. A seasoned leader carries a greater understanding of the kingdom of God and how to navigate spiritual warfare. When you are covered, you have a safe place to land when you're uncertain about the spiritual climates you will walk into. But here's where the wound of misunderstanding often comes in—when sons and daughters don't understand your *no*. They hear rejection when all you're trying to give is protection. They see limitations when you're offering preparation. It's one of the hardest parts of spiritual leadership—loving enough to correct, even when it isn't received as love.

I understand this well because I've been on the receiving end of a *no* myself. My husband, my covering, once told me no, and I remember how people reacted. Some thought he was trying to control me, to suppress the call of God on my life. But what he actually said was,

"Babe, there's going to come a day when I will be on one side of the world and you on the other, and I need to know that you will be spiritually sound and okay." That spoke volumes to my heart. His "no" wasn't about holding me back—it was about making sure I was ready.

There is something about hearing the word **"No"** that can feel like a storm rolling in out of nowhere. For many spiritual sons and daughters, receiving a **No** can feel like an abrupt shift from sunny skies to dark, looming clouds. And for spiritual parents, giving a **No** is not always easy either.

Eagerness to step out, even when a person believes they are ready shouldn't sway a leader to move emotionally. As a spiritual parent, you have to know that wisdom has to outweigh eagerness, preparation has to come before presentation, and divine timing has to take precedence over human excitement. But here's what I've learned—a "No" given in love and wisdom will calm the storm. The winds of disappointment may rage for a moment, the waves of misunderstanding may rise, but if the No is presented with clarity (the why), love, and wisdom, the waters will settle, and the relationship can move forward stronger than before, let me preface, if offensive don't set up in the heart of the recipient of the No.

So how do we position our hearts after the No? How do we make sure that correction is expressed through love, and how do we keep the lines of communication open to prevent wounds from festering into division?

Positioning Your Heart When You Receive a "No"

If you are a spiritual son or daughter, a "No" from a leader can sometimes feel personal. But I want to encourage you—No is not rejection. "No" is not punishment. "No" is not abandonment. A "No" is simply an opportunity to trust that God's wisdom is bigger than what you see in the moment. Here are three steps to position your heart when you receive a "No":

1. **Pause and Process Before Reacting**
   - Your first instinct may be to feel hurt, defensive, or even frustrated. That's normal. But take a moment to pause and process. Ask yourself:

   Is this No for my protection? Is this No because my

leader sees something I do not? Is this No preparing me for something greater?

- o Taking the time to reflect before responding can prevent offense and misunderstanding from taking root.

2. **Seek Understanding, Not Just Agreement**
    - o It's okay to ask for clarity. It's okay to have a conversation. But the goal should be to understand the wisdom behind the "No", not just to argue your perspective.
    - o Proverbs 4:7 reminds us, *"Wisdom is the principal thing; therefore, get wisdom: and with all thy getting get understanding."*
    - o If you can trust that your leader loves you, then you can also trust that they are guiding you with God's best in mind.

3. **Trust the Timing of God**
    - o Just because you received a No today does not mean the answer is No forever.
    - o Many times, a No is really a Not Yet—and in that waiting period (ask Barnabus), God is building, strengthening, and refining you.
    - o Trust that every delay is divine, and when the time is right, God will open the door in His perfect way. (Ask Joseph)

Davronia Val Scarbrough

How to Move Forward in Love and Clarity

If you are a spiritual leader, saying "No" is one of the hardest things to do, especially when you love the people you are leading, and you don't want to come across as a dictator. But I have learned that saying Yes to everything is not leadership, it is avoidance. True leadership requires wisdom, balance, and grace. (A moment of transparency here, there was a season when my husband and I said yes to everything, and it was the wrong thing to do.)

Here are three keyways to move forward in love and clarity after giving a "No":

1. **Communicate with Compassion, Not Control**
    - When delivering a "**No**", tone and approach matter. Instead of saying, *"No, you can't do that,"* explain the heart behind the decision.
    - A better way to approach it might be:
      "I see your passion, and I know you want to move forward, but I believe waiting will help you be even more prepared for what God is calling you to do."
    - Compassion in correction keeps relationships intact.

2. **Create a Pathway Forward**
    - A "No" should not be dead-end. Instead, it should be a redirection toward growth.
    - Offer guidance on what needs to happen next:
        a) "I believe a season of study and preparation will equip you for this next step."

       b) "Let's walk through this together so that when the time is right, you will be ready."
- This keeps the relationship open and builds trust rather than frustration.

3. **Reaffirm the Relationship**
   - A "No" should never feel like rejection. Make sure your spiritual son or daughter knows that their calling, growth, and purpose still matter to you.
   - Encourage them, speak life over them, and remind them that this moment is just a part of the process, not the end of it.
   - When love is evident, "No" does not feel like a dagger—it feels like guidance.

Stormy Seas Will Calm, and the Relationship Will Move Forward

Let's go back to the storm analogy. When a storm arises at sea, the waves crash, the winds howl, and it can feel chaotic and uncertain. This is why Jesus spoke to the wind and the waves and said, "Peace, be still." Why? Because without the element of peace resting, ruling, and abiding in the relationship, things can become chaotic, unstable, and easily destroyed by emotion rather than led by wisdom. When peace is absent, offense takes root. When peace is missing, misunderstandings linger longer than they should. When peace is not the foundation, correction feels like rejection, and love can be mistaken for control. Jesus didn't just calm the storm for the disciples' safety—He calmed the storm for their understanding. He was teaching them that external storms are inevitable, but the real battle is won when peace reigns internally.

And in spiritual relationships, we must have that same peace—a peace that anchors us in love even when the waves of misunderstanding rise, a peace that quiets the storms of offense, a peace that allows correction to be received without bitterness.

Because without peace, the waves of hurt, pride, and misunderstanding will continue to crash against the foundation of the relationship—until one day, what was meant to be a divine connection is completely washed away.

"My heart aches when this happens".

If a ship is steered with wisdom and patience, it will make it through the storm and sail into calm waters again.

The same is true in spiritual relationships. I know that sounds redundant, but I really want to drive this point home, because I have seen, and experienced God ordained relationships being washed away due to this two-letter word "No".

Let's move on.... A "No" may create temporary tension, but if the heart behind the "No" is love, wisdom, and clarity, the storm will pass. The relationship will grow stronger, trust will deepen, and what was once misunderstood will be seen with new eyes.

Jesus Himself had to tell His disciples "No" at times.

- When Peter tried to stop Him from going to the cross, Jesus rebuked him **(Matthew 16:23).**
- When the disciples wanted to call fire down on people, Jesus corrected them **(Luke 9:54-55).**

Yet, despite those "NOs", Jesus never rejected them, never abandoned them, and never stopped loving them.

That is the kind of leadership and mentorship we must model—one that is firm but loving, correcting but not condemning, guiding but never controlling.

CONCLUSION

If you are a spiritual son or daughter who has received a No, take a deep breath. It is not the end of the road. It is simply a part of the process. If you are a spiritual leader who has had to give a No, trust that if it is done with wisdom and love, the relationship will weather the storm and come out stronger.

At the end of the day, our goal is not just to say Yes to keep the peace. Our goal is to build, to grow, and to lead well.

And when No is given in love, with clear communication, and with a heart to see the other person thrive, it becomes a steppingstone, not a stumbling block.

Because the right "No" today can lead to the best "Yes" tomorrow.

Spiritual parenthood is a calling, but it comes with a cost. There will be moments of great joy and seasons of deep sorrow. Sons and daughters will come, and some will go. But our responsibility is to love them through it all, even if love is not returned.

But here's the good news: when love is the foundation, even the toughest lessons bear fruit in due time. The wounds of misunderstanding may linger for a season, but truth has a way of revealing itself.

Davronia Val Scarbrough

Journal Your Personal Prayer:

What Readers Are Saying…

As you read or listen, be prepared for a chapter that doesn't just inform—it transforms. "The Cost of Impartation" is not just another lesson in leadership, but a deeply revelatory and convicting word that speaks to the heart of every spiritual leader. The way Pastor Val exposes the subtle schemes and plots of the enemy to divide spiritual parents from their sons and daughters is both eye-opening and necessary. It is written with clarity and depth, but what sets it apart is the intention behind every line—to bring healing, understanding, and restoration.

This chapter caused me to pause and truly reflect on moments in ministry where I may have rushed, misjudged, or lacked patience. Questions filled my heart: Did I give her the time she needed? Was I gentle enough in my corrections? Could I have represented God's heart better? And that's what makes this chapter so impactful—it reminds us that if we are pastors after God's own heart, then our first priority must be servant leadership.

Only then will our calling reflect a life fully laid on the altar. Pastor Val masterfully balances practical insight with spiritual weight, making this chapter concise, clear, and powerfully moving.

Pastors Laurence & Chiquita Weathersby, Living The Word Int'l, Slidell, LA

Chapter Three

The Cost Of Impartation

The one thing about the place of parenting—whether in the natural or spiritual—is that a good parent always wants to give the best of what they have to offer. It's never about giving a child everything they want but rather equipping them with everything they need to succeed. Any loving father or mother in ministry desires to pour out wisdom, knowledge, and understanding so that their sons and daughters don't have to struggle unnecessarily. We want to see them thrive!

And this brings me to **Isaiah 49:23**, which reminds us of the divine role of spiritual parenting: *"Kings will be your foster fathers, and their queens, your nursing mothers. They will bow down before you with their faces to the ground; they will lick the dust at your feet. Then you will know that I am the LORD; those who hope in me will not be disappointed."* (**Isaiah 49:23, NIV**)

This is the divine structure of the kingdom—God has always established fathers and mothers to nurture, guide, and cover His people.

- **Kings as fathers**—those who lead with wisdom, who provide direction, protection, and spiritual authority.
- **Queens as mothers**—those who nourish, cultivate, and impart wisdom with grace and care.

And yes, there comes a day when a spiritual child will grow and venture out on their own—that's the goal of impartation. This should be what our heart desires.

But when a child leaves home *prematurely*, before they are truly prepared, it can lead to unnecessary hardships and missteps. I have seen it too many times and every time it hurts my heart. Sometimes, a few more months, a few more years, or even another decade of covering could have seasoned them to handle what they will inevitably face. But when impatience meets immaturity, it often leads to a painful departure and struggles/lessons that could have been avoided.

The Prodigal Pain

Take a trip with me for a moment. Let's revisit the story of the prodigal son—not just from the perspective of the son, but from that of the father. We don't hear about the mother in this passage, but let's imagine the weight that both parents carried as they watched their son walk away.

Can you see them sitting at the dinner table, whispering to each other about his immaturity? The father shaking his head, knowing his son lacked the wisdom to steward the inheritance he had just demanded? The mother sighing, concerned that her child was too naive, too trusting—easily manipulated by the world he was about to step into? Could you imagine the nights of intercession, the prayers lifted for his safety, for his return? Because here's what I believe; the prodigal son didn't just *come to himself* by accident.

The Bible says the father pondered the path, meaning he was watching and waiting. And that tells me something—he had an expectation. I truly believe his expectation was built on the foundation of prayer. He knew that despite his son's choices, despite his departure, despite his prodigal season, the prayers of a father and mother do not fall to the ground. He was confident that at some point, the very lessons he had imparted, the very truths he had spoken, would rise up in his son's spirit and lead him back home. And when that moment finally came, when he saw his son returning, the celebration wasn't just about his physical return—it was about answered prayers.

The Heart of the Older Brother

Now, I want to take a moment to visit the older brother in the prodigal's life. Many times, when spiritual children who have remained faithful to the vision and impartation see a celebration taking place for the one who seemingly didn't appreciate the gift of parents, it can stir up feelings of resentment. That fleeting voice I talked about earlier—the one that places a dagger in the hands of the most faithful—often begins to whisper: **"You stayed, you were loyal, and yet here they are being celebrated for coming back."**

The position of the older, faithful brother is tricky—and if not guarded by grace, it can become a dangerous place to be. Why do I say dangerous? Because it's easy to feel overlooked or unappreciated when others are being celebrated, especially those who seemed to have walked away with no appreciation for the blessing of spiritual covering. And if your heart isn't checked, faithfulness can quietly turn into frustration—and before you know it, you're standing there with a dagger in your hand, aimed at the very ones you were called to cover or celebrate. Remember the bible tells us, "the weapons of our warfare are not carnal but mighty in God for pulling down strongholds"

2 Corinthians 10:4 NKJV

Over the years, we have found it imperative to foster a prayer life in the "oldest" sons and daughters—to teach them how to pray not only for the safe return of those who have ventured away but also for their own hearts to remain pure. Jealousy and comparison are two of the enemy's most subtle weapons, and if left unchecked, they can create wounds just as deep as betrayal.

The Sacrifice of a Spiritual Parent

As spiritual parents, we often give the best of what we have, knowing that not everyone will fully appreciate it in the moment. We invest, we pour, we cover, we intercede—not for our own gain, but so that they can walk in the fullness of their calling. And yet, there are times when we watch them walk away, unprepared, full of zeal but lacking wisdom, taking with them everything we imparted without fully understanding its weight. That is the cost of impartation.

But like the father of the prodigal son, we must not lose hope. We must continue to pray, continue to believe, and continue to trust that what we have deposited in them will not be in vain. Because when they do come to themselves—when they finally realize the value of what they received, their return will not just be a moment of reconciliation. It will be a testimony of God's faithfulness, and of the power of impartation that never truly leaves them, no matter how far they go.

Conclusion

One of the most profound examples of true sonship is found in Jesus Himself. Even in His darkest moment, in the Garden of Gethsemane, when the weight of His assignment became unbearable, He never stopped calling God Father.

"Abba, Father," He said, "everything is possible for you. Take this cup from me. Yet not what I will, but what you will." (Mark 14:36)

Davronia Val Scarbrough

Even when He felt the sting of rejection on the cross, crying out, *"My God, my God, why have you forsaken me?"* (Matthew 27:46), He did not abandon His position as a son. He didn't walk away from the Father because the journey was painful. Instead, He surrendered to the will of the One who had sent Him.

This is the posture of true spiritual sonship and daughterhood. It is not about comfort—it is about commitment. It is not about how easy the journey is—it is about honoring the process, trusting the covering, and remaining faithful even when correction is hard to receive.

As spiritual parents, we must follow the example of the Father—correcting in love, leading with wisdom, and always keeping the door open for restoration. And as spiritual sons and daughters, we must follow the example of Jesus—honoring, submitting, and remaining faithful, even in seasons of discomfort.

Correction is never meant to break—it is meant to *build*. Love does not withhold truth; love *speaks* truth, even when it stings. And in the end, it is those who embrace correction, who yield to discipline, who remain even in the stretching—that will walk in the fullness of their calling.

The cost of impartation is great, but the reward is even greater. Stay the course. Honor the process. And never stop calling them *Father or Mother*.

Journal Your Personal Prayer:

Part Two

The Jewels—The Reward of Spiritual Fathering and Mothering

We've spent time addressing the daggers—the wounds, the misunderstandings, the betrayals that come with spiritual parenting. But let's shift now to *"the jewels"*.

Because while there is pain in this journey, there is also great reward. And that reward is seeing growth in those you've poured into. Seeing them embrace God's kingdom with maturity, honoring His statutes, ordinances, and principles—not out of obligation, but from a place of deep understanding. There is nothing like witnessing the spiritual fruit of your labor, knowing that the minutes, hours, days, and weeks invested into a life have yielded something *beautiful*.

This part of the book is about *that*—the joy of seeing sons and daughters return with wisdom, of witnessing their spiritual gifts flourish, and of receiving them with open arms when they come back with a greater understanding of what has been imparted to them.

What Readers Are Saying…

This chapter is a timely, Spirit-led exploration of a subject often tiptoed around in the Body of Christ—correction. Pastor Val handles it with a rare blend of prophetic boldness and pastoral compassion, delivering a message that is both convicting and healing. What makes this chapter so impactful is its ability to speak directly to the heart of spiritual parent-child relationships, addressing misunderstandings, misplaced offense, and the need to realign with God's divine structure. The repeated reminder that "Correction is not rejection" cannot be overstated—it is a truth that cuts through the confusion many spiritual sons and daughters wrestle with.

The comparison between Elisha's loyalty and Gehazi's opportunism serves as a powerful and sobering example of covenant versus conditional relationships. One of the most profound lines—"A title does not make someone a son. Submission does"—summarizes the heartbeat of this chapter. Pastor Val's teaching is deeply biblical, referencing the dynamics of Elijah and Elisha and grounded in the prophetic foundation of Isaiah 61.

This work stands apart from other writings by not only addressing spiritual authority, but shedding light on the heart and wisdom required to lead and follow well. As spiritual parents ourselves, we found this chapter to be a healing and clarifying tool that will help many navigate this sacred dynamic. This chapter is a necessary read for leaders and spiritual children alike.

Apostle Charles & Lady Charlette Perry,
Word of Restoration Int'l Church,
Rosharon, TX

Chapter Four

They Called You Father/Mother Until You Corrected Them

The Struggle with Correction

I thought writing this book would be painful, but in truth, with every chapter, I feel more love, understanding, and joy flood my heart. I can see beauty rising from the ashes, just as Isaiah 61:3 declares:

"To appoint unto them that mourn in Zion, to give unto them beauty for ashes, the oil of joy for mourning, the garment of praise for the spirit of heaviness; that they might be called trees of righteousness, the planting of the Lord, that he might be glorified."

Let's dive into the subject of "Correction". Correction is taboo. Correction is one of the hardest things for people to receive and talk about in the Body of Christ; yet it is also one of the greatest acts of love. The subject of correction can shift the winds in a matter of seconds. And where you were once called *father* or *mother*, you are now looked upon as clergy or preacher and the change is because you've had to bring correction. The moment guidance comes, many begin to resist, question, or even turn away. This isn't a new problem—it's an ancient one. The Bible speaks of the necessity of correction and wisdom:

> *"Hear, my sons, your father's instruction, and forsake not your mother's teaching."* (Proverbs 1:8)

There are lessons that only a father can instruct, and there are lessons that can only be learned from a mother's teaching. Both are necessary, yet many reject them. The structure of wisdom must be embraced again in the body of Christ.

What Is Correction Really?

Is correcting someone being mean-spirited? Is it an abuse of authority? Or is it, in reality, an act of deep love and admiration for the one God has entrusted into your care? God does nothing haphazardly—everything He does is intentional and precise. The crossing of paths between a spiritual parent and a spiritual child is not by chance; it is by divine design. This is the first thing both parties must acknowledge. A true covering is not something one stumbles into—it is something orchestrated by God in response to the prayers of a seeking heart. Let me pause here and say this: "some people have walked away from divine coverings only to place themselves in the hands of wolves". But that is a book for another time.

Back to what I was saying about *paths crossing*. If you have truly prayed for a covering, you must believe that God heard your prayer and answered you. Let's take a look at a powerful biblical example—***Elijah and Elisha.***

The Crossroad of Elijah and Elisha

Elijah was going about his journey when a moment in time everything changed. He found Elisha plowing in the field, and at the command of God, he cast his mantle upon him. This was no ordinary encounter—it was the beginning of a divine father-son relationship. Elisha had *many* opportunities to stop calling Elijah *father*. There were moments when Elijah seemingly pushed him away, telling him to stay behind while he moved forward. But Elisha refused to leave his side. Why? Because true sonship is not about convenience, it is about commitment. Imagine if Elisha had been offended by Elijah's ways. What if he had said, *"I thought you were my spiritual father, but now you're telling me to stay behind? Maybe you don't really care about me!"* But Elisha discerned something deeper. He understood that honor was not about comfort—it was about covenant.

This is where many spiritual sons and daughters falter. They are happy to receive impartation, favor, and opportunities under their covering, but the moment correction comes, their honor wavers.

Have We Rejected Wisdom?

I have a serious question for the body of Christ as a whole:

When did we find it unnecessary to heed the voice of wisdom?

Have we allowed the *Babylonian* system to become so ingrained in our hearts that we now find the voice of God—the voice of the Holy Spirit—to be nonsensical, outdated, or irrelevant?

See, when I talk about a *Babylonian system*, I'm talking about a mindset and way of life that is void of God. A system that exalts personal ambition over submission. A system that prioritizes self over sacrifice. A system that believes it can function in the kingdom without guidance. But that is so far from God's ways.

God has always established **fathers and mothers** as a strategic part of His divine structure.

They are carriers of wisdom, protectors of inheritance, and stewards of spiritual mantles.

Isaiah 49:23 (NIV) declares:

"Kings will be your foster fathers, and their queens your nursing mothers."

This is a divine order. God intended for leadership to be nurtured, instructed, and covered. But when we reject spiritual fatherhood and motherhood, we cut ourselves off from the very system God designed to equip and sustain us.

The Devil Hates Submission

Submission has to be repackaged in the body of Christ. The reason the enemy has worked so hard to place a negative connotation on submission is because he himself never felt the need to submit—not to wisdom, love, grace, hierarchy, or kingdom structure.

The enemy thrives on rebellion. He is always before the throne of God, pointing out the moments when we resist divine authority.

He lives to accuse the brethren, to show God a report card filled with our failures in submission and obedience.

Do not give him that satisfaction.

Gehazi: When Honor Is Conditional

Since we are discussing Elijah and Elisha, let's shift our focus for a moment to Elisha's own journey in fathering Gehazi. Unlike Elisha, Gehazi struggled with correction. He wanted impartation, but not discipline. He wanted the benefits of sonship, but not the responsibilities. His story is a tragic one because **his honor was conditional**. He stayed close as long as it benefited him, but the moment greed and pride took root, his true heart was revealed.

When Elisha confronted him about his deception regarding Naaman's gifts, Gehazi did not receive correction—he rejected it. And because of that rejection, he inherited a curse instead of a blessing.

This is a cautionary tale. True spiritual inheritance is not just passed down; it is received through humility and obedience. It is not given to those who demand it, but to those who honor it.

The Heart of True Sonship

True sonship and daughterhood are not claimed by words—they are *proven* through action.

- A title does not make someone a son. **Submission does.**
- A position does not make someone a leader. **Character does.**

Jesus Himself showed us this. Though He was equal with God, He **submitted** to the will of the Father. He never operated outside of His covering. He walked in obedience, even when it was painful.

As spiritual parents, we carry the weight of raising sons and daughters in the faith, knowing that some will receive correction with humility and grow, while others will reject it and walk away. But regardless of the outcome, our role remains the same:

- We must teach.
- We must guide.
- We must lead in love.

Because, at the end of the day, fatherhood and motherhood in the spirit are not positions of control, but positions of stewardship.

Conclusion

The structure of wisdom must be restored.

We must return to the foundational truths that fathers instruct, and mothers teach. And we must recognize that correction is not rejection, it is an invitation to growth. To those who struggle with correction, I encourage you—do not forsake the voice of wisdom.

Because true sons and daughters are not just those who receive the blessing, but those who remain even when discipline comes.

Remember This:

Correction is not rejection. Correction is not control. Correction is an act of love. A wise son or daughter will recognize that. And when they do, they will walk in the fullness of their calling—untainted, unshaken, and truly prepared for the weight of the mantle they are meant to carry.

Journal Your Personal Prayer:

Davronia Val Scarbrough

What Readers Are Saying...

*T*he topic of spiritual fathers and mothers to sons and daughters is one that is rarely explored in depth, which makes *"You Got the Jewels, I Got the Dagger"* both timely and necessary. The chapter we reviewed was not only easy to read and understand, but it also went straight to the heart of the matter, offering insight into a sometimes volatile yet sacred dynamic. What stood out most was the way the author clearly defines the responsibilities of spiritual parents—mentorship, love, correction, guidance, and the passing on of faith and wisdom.

*P*astor Val reminds us that spiritual parenting is a divine calling, and when carried out with the heart of God, the labor is never in vain. Using real-life experiences and relatable examples, she mirrors the natural parent-child relationship to demonstrate the value and beauty of the spiritual one. The clarity and compassion in which this chapter is written make it a valuable tool for both those actively serving in spiritual parenting roles and those who seek to honor and understand them.

*W*e highly recommend this book to all spiritual fathers, mothers, sons, and daughters. It brings understanding, encouragement, and honor to a relationship that is often misunderstood, yet deeply impactful to the growth and unity of the Body of Christ.

Bishop Osco & First Lady Gardin, Elizabeth Missionary Baptist Church, Monroe, NC

Chapter Five

When Sons and Daughters Return with Wisdom

The Joy of Seeing Growth

There is nothing like watching someone you've spiritually parented come into their own—when they no longer just repeat what they've been taught but understand it, apply it, and live it. When they begin to see the kingdom the way you do, to grasp the weight of divine order, and to walk in honor, authority, and wisdom. I want to pause here and give a testimony of how serious I—no, *we*—take the position of spiritual parenting. We didn't *ask* for this, but we were *graced* for it.

Ezekiel 16:1-10 paints a powerful picture of God's love and restoration. It describes how He saw me in my mess, in my brokenness—unable to get it right if you paid me to. And yet, He covered me. He nurtured me. He waited until the appointed time and then adorned me with His love. Why? Because He knew that one day, I would be able to feed and nurture others.

What an *honor*.

That's why this work is so important. It's not about control. It's about stewardship. It's about seeing beyond where someone is and into who they are called to be.

Davronia Val Scarbrough

A Moment of Growth

I remember a conversation with one of my spiritual daughters—a conversation that lasted a solid two hours. She said something that shook me:

"I see the error of my behavior. Either you will grow, or what God has given you to do will dry up."

Powerful.

See, at that moment, I realized she had caught it. She didn't just hear what I'd been teaching, she *saw* it. She had come into the understanding that growth is not just about gifting; it's about character, stewardship, and submission. It was one of those moments where I felt the weight of the responsibility God had placed in my hands, but also the beauty of seeing someone I had poured into turn around and pour back into me.

The Gift of Mutual Encouragement

Honestly, I now thoroughly enjoy the conversations I have with my spiritual daughters. No, they are not all in the same place of growth, but when I see the growth, it blesses me beyond words. It blesses me that they turn around and bless me—with wisdom, with encouragement, and with strength. And that's why I didn't want this book to just be about *the daggers* that went in my back. Because if the truth be told, I serve the master physician. He knows how to mend, remove, and care for me. I *know* I'm going to be alright because I stand on this truth: *"I know whom I have believed and am persuaded that he is able to keep that which I have committed unto him against that day."* **(2 Timothy 1:12 NKJV)**

I trust that every seed I have sown, every lesson I have given, every tear I have cried over a son or daughter—it is all kept by God.

Conclusion

If you're a spiritual parent, hold on. The work is not in vain. Some will walk away. Some will misunderstand you. But some—*some*—will come back with wisdom. Some will return with the jewels of understanding, and when they do, you will see the beauty that came out of what once felt like ashes.

If you're a spiritual son or daughter, trust the process. Even when it doesn't make sense. Even when correction stings. Know that God places coverings in your life not to control you, but to prepare you.

And for both sides—when the moment comes where wisdom meets understanding, where the one who was poured into returns with maturity, and where love is given and received in its fullness—that is when the jewels of spiritual parenthood truly shine.

Davronia Val Scarbrough

Journal Your Personal Prayer:

What Readers Are Saying...

It was both a joy and an inspiration to read and listen to the portion of *"You Got the Jewels, I Got the Dagger"* assigned to me. Chapter Six: "Spiritual Legacy – What You Build Will Outlive You" stands as more than a reflection—it is a powerful declaration and goal for every spiritual leader. I deeply appreciate that the chapter is framed as an affirmation, reminding us that our calling is not for the moment, but for the generations to come.

The entire chapter was impactful to me. It challenged me to pause and reflect: Am I truly investing in others for the sake of Kingdom building, or am I simply doing it out of routine? That question pierced my heart in the best way, pushing me to evaluate the intentionality behind my mentorship. It also stirred deep gratitude within me for the spiritual giants who poured into my life, especially the late Dr. Willie C. Jones. Although he has transitioned his legacy continues to live through me, shaping the way I lead and mentor others today.

Pastor Val's passion for this subject radiates throughout the chapter. Her words are not only thoughtful and biblically grounded, but they serve as a timely reminder that true spiritual parenting is legacy work. Pastor Val, you have done an outstanding job, and this work is a much-needed voice in the Body of Christ.

Bishop Marvin Frank Thomas, Sr.
Presiding Prelate First Episcopal District CME
Memphis, TN

Chapter Six
Spiritual Legacy – What You Build Will Outlive You

- The Goal of Every Father/Mother: Reproduction in the Spirit
- Sons and Daughters as an Extension of Your Ministry
- Raising Leaders, Not Dependents

Building Beyond Your Lifetime

Okay, let's put it out there in the open... every leader, parent—spiritual and natural—teacher, evangelist, pastor, and apostle should be building their portion of the kingdom in a way that outlives them.

The Bible tells us in Genesis 12:2 NKJV that God made Abraham a promise:

"I will make your name great, and you will be a blessing."

But here's the thing—God wasn't just talking about making Abraham's name great for that moment in time. No, Abraham's name is still great today because he allowed God to guide him as he led. His obedience, his faith, and his legacy extended beyond his physical years on earth. So, I have a question for every leader, every spiritual parent:

"What will your eulogy sound like out of the mouths of those God has entrusted into your hands?"

I often tell my spiritual daughters in our personal times of fellowship, travel, and ministry, "When you stand over me one day, this is what I want to be said." Why? Because my desire is that the wisdom I impart into others will far outlive the days I spend here on earth.

The Example of My Grandmother

Let me give you a real-life example of what I mean. My grandmother—one of my heroes in the faith—left behind a legacy so rich that, at her funeral, people came from as far as California, South Carolina, North Carolina, Georgia, and her local community to honor her. One after the other, they stood and spoke about how she had taught them the Word of God, how she had poured into their lives, corrected them with love, and imparted wisdom that changed them forever. There were *so many* pastors on the pulpit that day—men and women who had been shaped by a 5'4" woman whose impact far exceeded her physical stature.

That's what legacy looks like. That's what it means for your name to outlive your years.

There is a poem that asks, *"How will you live your dash?"* That dash—the time between your birth and your departure—is all you have to make an impact. As spiritual parents in the body of Christ, this question should always resonate at the forefront of our existence.

Jesus and the Ultimate Spiritual Legacy

I love the scripture where Jesus says:

"I am going away..." (John 14:2-3)

I hear so much in that statement.

- I hear, It's in your hands now.
- I hear, this baton is precious—steward it well.

- I hear, Yes, crucifixion will come but be of good courage—your name will outlive the nails, the stake, and the thorns.

Jesus was telling His disciples that His time on earth was coming to an end, but the work wasn't finished. It was now their responsibility to carry it forward. That is legacy. That is spiritual parenting at its highest level. It's not just about teaching people; it's about equipping them to lead in your absence.

That's why the focus of spiritual parenthood should always be on raising leaders, not dependents. The sons and daughters we nurture should not only grow in wisdom but also extend the reach of the kingdom.

Jewels Are Forever

It's easy to get caught up in the wounds—the daggers, the disappointments, the betrayals—but daggers are temporal, jewels are forever. At the end of it all, what matters most is not the daggers we've endured, but the legacy we leave behind. The enemy would love for us to focus on who hurt us, but God wants us to focus on who we've built up. So, concentrate on your name and the legacy attached to your faithfulness to the assignment. One day, when it's time to pass the baton, may the jewels of wisdom, impartation, and faith far outweigh the wounds. Because that—the spiritual legacy we leave behind—is what will truly outlive us.

Conclusion

When all is said and done, what will be remembered? Will it be temporary pain, or will it be the eternal impact? Jesus endured the cross knowing that the suffering was temporary, but the fruit of His obedience would be eternal.

As spiritual parents, may we do the same—raising up sons and daughters who will carry the torch long after we are gone. Because if we build well, if we pour wisely, and if we remain faithful to the call, the work of our hands will never die. Legacy is not about how many years we live—it's about who carries our name and our wisdom into the next generation.

Davronia Val Scarbrough

Journal Your Personal Prayer:

What Readers Are Saying...

Relationships are, in our opinion, the number one area of life that the enemy attacks the most. He knows you can't get purpose right and get relationships wrong. Relationships and purposes go hand in hand. Our relationship with God, our spouse, friends and family affect purpose. The Bible says, if a man does not know how to rule his own house, how will he take care the church of God? In other words, if a man doesn't know how to do relationships at home how shall he succeed in his assignment. The Relationship of Spiritual parenting has been misunderstood for a very long time. And yet we see Biblical examples, Elisha referring to Elijah as his father and Paul referring to Timothy as a son. And Peter refers to Mark as a son. In Val's book "You Got the Jewels, but I got the Dagger" offers great insight on how to understand the dynamics of that relationship and bring healing, commitment and mutual respect. Everything that God does He does it through divine connections. God's goal for these relationships is to help you go to the next level. Some of your greatest gifts will walk into your life as friends and spiritual parents. "There is a friend that sticks closer than a brother." So, what you miss in natural family — God will supplement in spiritual family. Relationships take honor, trust, commitment and character on the part of the children as well as the spiritual parents. How we relate to one another is essential. Hebrews 13:17 "Obey your spiritual leaders and do what they say.

Their work is to watch over your souls, and they are accountable to God. Give them reason to do this with joy and not with sorrow. That would certainly not be for your benefit." The benefits should be for the whole, Fathers and Sons - both will profit.

Davronia Val Scarbrough

*B*eing in the position of being spiritual son and daughter to our spiritual parents and having the oversight of being spiritual parents to so many, we understand sonship and parenting. The contents of this book help you to understand, it's not just about who you are over but who you are under. The evil spirit answered and said, Jesus I know, and Paul I know; but who are you? Acts19:15 Jesus and Paul were under the authority of the Father and their relationship produced power. Whatever position you may be in whether a spiritual son or daughter or spiritual parents this book will cause you to look at your relationship and reflect on the relationship that Jesus wants to have with us. His relationship with the Father allows us to see God wants to be to us and so we know what we can be to others in our relationships.

Apostles Tony and Cynthia Brazelton
Victory Christian Ministries International
Spiritual Parents of Pastors Eddie & Val Scarbrough

Chapter Seven

True Sonship Is Proven, Not Just Claimed

Title vs. Action—The True Test of Sonship

Let's dive into a serious question. Leader, are you a good example of sonship or daughtership?

I ask this because too often, people desire the title of a son or daughter, but they have never been proven. And a title without testing is a disaster waiting to happen. Let me pause right here—because I don't want this to be misunderstood. You can be a great spiritual child, sow seeds of honor, and walk in integrity, yet when you are placed in a position of spiritual authority, you may still get the worst dagger ever. "Ask Elisha".

Elisha was one of the most faithful spiritual sons in Scripture. He followed Elijah relentlessly, honored his every word, and refused to leave his side. Yet, when Elisha became the spiritual father to Gehazi, he experienced dishonor firsthand. Gehazi, his spiritual son, rejected his wisdom, ran after riches, and ultimately paid the price for his rebellion. Elisha never sowed dishonor, yet he experienced it from his own son.

This is a hard truth in spiritual leadership. Just because you honor well doesn't mean those who follow you will do the same.

And here's another hard truth: you may not always understand the decisions your spiritual parents make, the way they move, or the questions they pose. But that does not mean they are wrong.

I know this personally because of our relationship with our spiritual covering, Apostle Tony and Cynthia Brazelton.

There were many times we may not have fully understood why they said what they said. We may not have fully grasped the correction that was given or the direction that was laid before us. But here's what we did know: "our relationship with them was for life."

We knew it wasn't a coincidence that our lives collided for the sake of the kingdom. And that understanding anchored us, even when we didn't have all the answers.

That's the heart of true sonship. You don't have to understand everything to remain faithful. You just have to trust that divine connections are orchestrated by God—and that He places coverings in our lives for a purpose.

True Sonship: More Than a Title

There is a huge difference between claiming sonship and proving it.

A person can call someone their spiritual father or mother all day long, but if their actions don't align with that claim, the title means nothing. Sonship is not just about proximity; it is about posture. It is about honor, submission, and trust—even when correction comes.

Jesus showed us the perfect example of this. Though He was equal with God, He submitted to the will of the Father. He never acted outside of His Father's authority. He never rebelled. He never tried to do His own thing apart from God's plan. Instead, He said:

"I do nothing on My own initiative, but I speak these things as the Father taught Me." (John 8:2 NLT)

That is the heart of a true son—one who does not just carry the *name* of their father but the nature of their father.

Recognizing Those Who Are Truly Connected

When you are truly connected to your spiritual leadership, your words, actions, and mindset will reflect it. Let's look at Elisha again.

When Elijah was about to be taken up, the other prophets came to Elisha and repeatedly said, *"You know your father is going to leave you today, right?"*

The greatest sermon Elisha ever preached, in my opinion, was found in his response:

"Be quiet." (2 Kings 2:3)

That was it.

Be quiet.

Why? Because true sonship doesn't entertain distractions. True sonship doesn't engage in unnecessary conversations that question or undermine their covering. True sonship stays focused on the assignment, refusing to be pulled into speculation, division, or emotional distractions. Elisha knew what was about to happen. He didn't need *outside voices* feeding him doubt or fear. He was *locked in*. He stayed close. He kept his eyes on his father. And because of that, he *received the double portion*.

Conclusion

Sonship is not in what you say—it's in how you serve, how you honor, and how you remain steadfast, even when the season changes.

A title does not make you a son. **Faithfulness does.**

A position does not make you a leader. **Character does.**

Elisha walked out his sonship with action. He stayed when others stood at a distance. He focused when others whispered. And because of that, he inherited something greater than a title—he inherited a *mantle*.

Davronia Val Scarbrough

So, I leave you with this question: Are you just carrying a name, or are you carrying a nature? Because true sonship is not claimed—it is proven.

Journal Your Personal Prayer:

_____
_____
_____
_____
_____
_____
_____
_____
_____
_____
_____
_____
_____
_____
_____
_____
_____
_____
_____.

You Got The Jewels But I Got The Dagger

Part Three

Davronia Val Scarbrough

What Readers Are Saying...

My overall opinion of this chapter is it's a masterpiece.

..."simply because every one of us in ministry has found ourselves in situations where it is necessary to seek help in dealing with the ugliness of betrayal"

"This chapter is quite inspiring, highlighting what causes leaders to inflict pain on themselves and perpetuate it further. The author does a fine job of offering valuable insights into the benefits of healing, growing, surviving, and thriving after betrayal with an unoffended heart."

"Loving Beyond Betrayal". This chapter is brilliantly written and very relatable to her intended audience. It's a given that spiritual parents, leaders, as well as spiritual sons and daughters, will be wounded in the line of duty.

If you have ever experienced the pain of betrayal or helped someone navigate it, this book is sure to guide and inspire you epically. Of all the books dealing with forgiveness and betrayal, this chapter was particularly poignant and resonates with me, as I have had to navigate such experiences and are not exempt from future betrayals.

*L*oving beyond betrayal requires education and a willingness to put in the work; the tips and tools are provided in this book. If you're interested in effectively leading while navigating the inevitableness of betrayal, this is the book for you to read.

Thank you, Pastor Val Scarbrough

Dr. C. Rumph-Anderson, Rochester, NY

Chapter Eight

Loving Beyond Betrayal

The Opportunity to Be Offended

I would be remiss if I didn't state the obvious: as a spiritual leader, you will be presented by the devil with the opportunity to be offended.

When hurt is part of the equation, it is so easy—almost natural—to open your heart up to offense. It's the response the enemy wants you to have. It's his way of trapping you, keeping you focused on the pain instead of the purpose.

Now, I'm quite sure that some of the people who walked away will buy a copy of this book. And to you, I say: ***Thank you for your support of the ministry.***

But let me be clear—at our separation, I was presented with the opportunity to be offended, and so were you. But I had to pass up on that opportunity.

Why?

Because I live my life with this one guiding thought:

"I never know if God will use me to speak into that person's life again." That means I had to, many times—kicking and screaming, with tears streaming down my face—remove the dagger, lay it at the feet of Jesus, and totally surrender my heart to agape love. And with every wound, I had to say, "Father, forgive them, for they know not what they do." (Luke 23:34 ASV)

But let's be real—forgiveness does not excuse bad behavior. It does not mean that abuse should ever be tolerated. But what it does mean is that I refuse to let malice, bitterness, or resentment take root in my heart. Because here's the truth: God has a way of <u>testing you</u> in the middle of a mess. Ask me how I know? I Can't Afford to Be Offended—And Neither Can You I have too much to do in the kingdom to be offended. And so do you.

Paul talks about in **2 Corinthians 2:10-11** what offense does to the church. He warns us that unforgiveness gives Satan an advantage over us. Think about that—offense doesn't just hurt you; it actually gives the enemy a foothold to operate in the body of Christ.

That's why I can't hold onto offense. That's why I refuse to stay in the place of hurt. Because daggers are formed by the enemy to kill you. But the Bible tells us: "No weapon formed against you shall prosper." (Isaiah 54:17 NKJV)

That's why concentrating on the hurt is dangerous—it gives power to the weapon that was formed. But when you refuse to walk in offense—when you choose instead to walk in love—you shift the power back into God's hands. His love will cover you, and His love will cover and correct them. I must trust that. And so do you.

Conclusion

At the end of the day, walking in love is a choice.

It's not easy. It's not always fair. But it is always necessary.

So, if you've been hurt, if you've had daggers thrown your way, if you've been presented with the opportunity to be offended, I challenge you to pass it up. Choose love. Choose healing.

Choose to believe that God's justice is greater than your need for vindication.

Because in the end, offense is a trap. The assignment we carry in the Kingdom is far too important for us to be entangled by offense, bitterness, or unresolved wounds. We can't afford to be distracted by what was done to us, when there's so much God still wants to do through us. The weight of our calling demands clear hearts, clean hands, and focused minds—because souls are on the line, legacies are being shaped, and eternity is being impacted by our obedience. Simply put, the work is too great, and the cost of staying offended is far too high.

Davronia Val Scarbrough

Journal Your Personal Prayer:

Maturity – based on slow careful consideration having completed natural growth and development: ripe, having undergone maturation: having attained a final or desired state

Davronia Val Scarbrough

What Readers Are Saying...

*P*astor Val has truly written an impactful and heart-searching work that speaks deeply to the journey of spiritual leadership and mentorship. I thoroughly enjoyed my chapter—so much so that I listened to it twice! The concept is powerful, and the message resonates with a depth that's rarely explored in this way. One of the most memorable and thought-provoking truths was the reminder that "they may not see the value until later in life"—yet we're still called to impart, knowing we're sowing for their future. The ability to let go while still pouring out is both freeing and sobering. The line "God has ownership, we have partnership" was especially impactful, reminding me that my responsibility is to impart in obedience, not to control the outcome. The narrative was structured with great clarity and flow, making it easy to follow while leaving a lasting impression. This is a much needed and rare conversation, and I believe it will bless and shift hearts across generations.

Pastor S. Motley, Radical Faith Church, Danville, VA

Chapter Nine
How Precious Are the Jewels to You?

Leaving Their Hearts in God's Hands

At some point, we must release those we've poured into. Whether they recognize the value of what they received now or later, their journey is ultimately between them and God.

Letting go doesn't mean we stop loving—it means we trust that God's process will do what our words and efforts cannot.

But how do we surrender our spiritual sons and daughters to God without bitterness or regret?

That's the real test.

It's one thing to release someone physically—it's another thing to release them emotionally and spiritually. Sometimes, we say we've let go, but deep down, we're still holding onto disappointment, frustration, or the lingering question: Did I waste my time?

That's where trust comes in.

Trust that every seed sown will bear fruit somewhere. Trust that every lesson given will take root at the appointed time. Trust that even if they walked away from you, they cannot walk away from what God has deposited in them through you.

How Do You See the Jewels?

Here's an even deeper question: How do you see the jewels? Do you see them through the eyes of possessiveness—as something you own, something you control, something that is owed back to you?

Or do you see them through the lens of freely I have received, freely I give? The way you frame what has been so richly and freely given to you by God is the same way you will release it to others. If you hold onto the jewels with pride, thinking they are yours to distribute as you see fit, you will feel entitled to something in return. And when people walk away without acknowledging their value, you will feel robbed. But when you recognize that everything—every ounce of wisdom, every moment of revelation, every word of truth—was given to you not for ownership but for stewardship, you will learn to give without expectation of return. That's where freedom is.

The Power of Freely Giving

Let me share something personal.

I spend a lot of alone time—praying, listening to the voice of God, studying, reading, or absorbing teachings from others. I can literally get lost in my personal relationship with the Trinity. I know that time spent with Jesus yields great benefits and wisdom, but here's what I've come to understand: "The wisdom He imparts to me isn't for me to become the guru of spiritual truths."

It's for me to *freely give* to others.

This is how you truly value "the jewels"—not by hoarding them, not by measuring their worth by who receives them, but by pouring them out as an act of obedience and love. One thing I know for sure—there is an expiration date of my life here. But there is ***no expiration date*** on the jewels God has given me. I have seven natural grandchildren as I write this book, and it is my prayer that I deposit something in them that will solidify their walk with God. But I also have several spiritual sons and daughters, and my prayer is that the jewels I release to them will be just as infallible, unshakable, and enduring.

I stand on **2 Corinthians 4:2**:

"But we have renounced the hidden things of dishonesty, not walking in craftiness, nor handling the word of God deceitfully; but by manifestation of the truth commending ourselves to every man's conscience in the sight of God."

What	we	*say*	matters.
How	we	*lead*	matters.
How	we	*steward*	matters.

How we develop our spiritual sons and daughters matters.

The jewels we release are not just for now—they are for eternity.

Conclusion

This chapter challenges us to ask: Do we value the jewels enough to give them freely, even when they are not appreciated? Because the true worth of the jewels we impart is not determined by who receives them, but by the eternal impact they carry. The jewels are not for our glory, they are for His. So, we must release them freely. We must trust God with the ones who walk away. We must continue to pour, even when the cup we poured into is no longer in front of us. Because the jewels will outlive us. And that, my friend, is the real reward.

Davronia Val Scarbrough

Journal Your Personal Prayer:

What Readers Are Saying...

This chapter is a powerful and heartfelt exploration of the impact and eternal value of spiritual legacy. It beautifully highlights the sacred relationship between the spiritual leader and those who are seeking to grow closer to the Father, emphasizing that the journey is both personal and shared. What makes this work truly exceptional is its realistic portrayal of the spiritual path—the highs, the missteps, and the grace that meets us in every part of the process. The authors noted how deeply meaningful it was to see the honest acknowledgment that even spiritual leaders stumble, but God still uses those faltering steps to open doors and continue impartation. The chapter is made even richer by the biblical reflections on legacy through the lives of Abraham, Isaac, Jacob, David, and Esther—a reminder that our influence should endure beyond our time. With a clear, thoughtful structure, this chapter empowers mentors and uplifts those being mentored, nurturing both with truth and grace. Ultimately, it leaves you with this undeniable truth: the greatest seed a spiritual leader can plant is the love of Christ—eternal and transformative.

Andrew B. Smoke & First Lady Patricia Smoke
Presiding-Elder Charlotte District AME Zion Church

Chapter Ten

The Joy of Spiritual Legacy Flourishing Sons, Daughters & Heavenly Rewards

A Journey of Reflection and Celebration

The journey of this book has been one of reflection, appreciation, rededication, optimism, and trust. Each word represents an emotion or declaration that has shaped this process.

Reflection, because I've taken the time to look back on the beauty and challenges of spiritual parenting.

Appreciation, because I am grateful for the opportunity to serve, to lead, and to love.

Rededication, because I reaffirm my commitment to raising and stewarding sons and daughters in the kingdom.

Optimism, because I choose to believe that this relationship, when done properly, will always bear fruit.

Trust, because I know that God is in control of every relationship—those that flourished and those that fell apart.

I want my journey to be meaningful, who doesn't?

But more than that, I didn't want us to take this journey together only to end up in a place of doom and gloom, with a negative light cast on the body of Christ.

That was never the goal.

No, I wanted this journey to expose the enemy for who he is and what he does to relationships.

And now? It's time to celebrate!

The Power and Joy of Spiritual Legacy

Kingdom order is powerful when done properly.

It's impactful when managed with wisdom and integrity.

And the rewards are great when we understand roles and seasons.

There is joy in spiritual legacy.

- Abraham found joy in his legacy.
- Isaac found joy in his legacy.
- Jacob found joy in his legacy.
- David found joy in his legacy.
- Esther found joy and reward in her legacy.

And we could go throughout the Bible, finding so many more who stewarded the spiritual parent and spiritual child relationship well—and through it, the kingdom of God advanced.

The joy of spiritual parenting is knowing that what you have sown will outlive you. That the time you poured, the prayers you covered them with, the wisdom you imparted—it will not return void.

This is why we must celebrate, not lament.

The Beauty of This Relationship

I really want to walk away from this book expressing the beauty of this relationship.

I know the title may have piqued your curiosity—because let's be honest, people are drawn to stories of pain. Some psychologists say it's because hearing about the struggles of others makes people feel better about their own lives or situations.

But I didn't write this book just to tell *painful* stories.

I wanted to:

- Expose the pain, yes.
- Expose the hurt, absolutely.
- But most importantly, **expose the enemy's lies**—his deception, his schemes, and his desire to destroy this divine relationship between spiritual parents and children.

Because the enemy knows this:

"Two will put ten thousand to flight." (Deuteronomy 32:30)
He knows that when this relationship is in order, the kingdom advances.

He knows that when spiritual fathers and mothers raise up sons and daughters with wisdom, love, and truth, strongholds are broken, generations are shifted, and mantles are passed properly.

So, my friend, there is joy in spiritual legacy.

You and I—we are the harvest of someone else's time, labor, and love. Someone poured into us. Someone prayed for us. Someone fought for our development. And now, we get to do the same for others.

But what we must never forget is this:

Our *heavenly reward* awaits.

When we glorify the kingdom through these relationships—when we honor and steward well—there is a reward beyond what we can imagine.

At the end of it all, I pray that your journey as a spiritual parent grows sweeter and sweeter, and your journey as a spiritual son or daughter grows stronger and stronger. Because at the end of the day, we all long to hear these words from our Father:

"Well done, thy good and faithful servant." (Matthew 25:21 NLT)

Conclusion

And so, this is where we end—but it's not really an ending, is it?

This is just the beginning of a deeper awareness of the jewels we carry, the relationships we cultivate, and the impact we leave behind.

May we steward well.

May we love deeply.

May we leave a legacy that outlives us.

Because the greatest joy of all is not just seeing sons and daughters flourish on earth—it's knowing that our work has been sealed in heaven. And there is no greater reward than that!

Davronia Val Scarbrough

Journal Your Personal Prayer:

What Readers Are Saying...

This chapter offers a refreshing level of transparency and accountability from the spiritual parenthood perspective, a viewpoint that is often neglected in similar works. Unlike many books that primarily address the journey of spiritual sons and daughters, *"You Got the Jewels, I Got the Dagger"* intentionally centers the role, responsibility, and heart of the spiritual parent. It identifies the areas that leaders must build, strengthen, and steward well in order to cultivate healthy, lasting spiritual relationships.

One of the most powerful truths that stood out is the idea that spiritual parenting should always focus on raising leaders, not dependents. That mindset shift is vital for the Body of Christ and offers a model of mentorship that empowers, rather than enables.

This is a book that is timely, insightful, inspiring, and filled with the wealth and wisdom of Almighty God. The well-written words, clearly guided by the Holy Spirit, have the power to bring healing, wholeness, and freedom to the Church. It speaks to the importance of legacy—not just in name, but in the transfer of godly wisdom to the next generation.

The narrative is clear, compelling, and deeply impactful. Every reader, whether a spiritual parent or child, will walk away strengthened, equipped, and richly blessed.

Pastor Michelle Turner
Faith Soldiers Word Ministries, Charlotte, NC

Chapter Eleven

The Gift of Spiritual Motherhood—Lessons from Ruth and Naomi

I would be remiss as a woman in ministry if I did not take a moment to speak about one of the most profound spiritual mother-daughter relationships in the Bible—Ruth and Naomi. Their journey together was not just about survival; it was about faith, trust, mentorship, and divine alignment. But before I go any further, I want to make this disclaimer: "I have been blessed with beautiful, God-fearing, and loving women in my life who have invited me into their personal space." Yes, I said invited me into their life space—because not all spiritual sons and daughters are first seen by leadership. Some are drawn in by divine connection and invite themselves into the space of mentorship.

Yes, we must pray about who we are to mentor, but let's be clear—it is a privilege to be invited into the lives of others. It is an honor that they trust the wisdom God has given us for this position.

And with that being said, I have learned that women are deeply relational. The way we build connections, invest in relationships, and create spaces of trust is very different from the way men do.

And because of that, navigating the spiritual assignment of being a mother in ministry requires great discernment—especially when it comes to boundaries.

The Fine Line of Spiritual Motherhood

This is the tricky part.

Relationships matter. Building trust, mutual respect, and integrity makes all the difference. But here's the challenge: When both parties are deeply invested, a lot of time is spent in each other's presence. Conversations become frequent, personal stories are shared, victories and struggles are celebrated together—and in that closeness, you have to know what is safe and what removes the necessary boundaries.

I want to speak from personal experience.

There were times when I became too familiar with the personal lives of those I mentored, and it caused missteps in the relationship. My intentions were pure—I wanted to guide, to uplift, to support—but there is a right way and a wrong way to lead. The right way is grounded in wisdom, accountability, and spiritual discernment.

The wrong way? It is blurred by over-involvement, emotional entanglement, and misplaced roles. I had to learn that not every part of someone's journey requires my presence, only my prayers. This is where Ruth and Naomi's relationship speaks volumes.

Ruth and Naomi—A Blueprint for Spiritual Mothers and Daughters

Ruth and Naomi's story was not just about family, it was about mentorship, faith, and divine alignment. Yes, Naomi guided Ruth in the natural—teaching her the customs of Israel, advising her on how to position herself for her future, and helping her navigate difficult transitions. But the spiritual aspect of their relationship ran even deeper.

Naomi introduced Ruth to a new belief system—one that centered around faith in the One True God. Naomi modeled strength, wisdom, and resilience, teaching Ruth how to walk by faith and not by sight.

Naomi provided guidance and covering, helping Ruth move in wisdom and obedience as she stepped into her destiny. Most importantly, their relationship brought comfort, love, and purpose—it was a divine connection ordained by God. This is what true spiritual motherhood looks like. It is not just about sharing wisdom; it is about helping someone step fully into who God created them to be.

Ruth's Perspective: The Heart of a Spiritual Daughter

I imagine Ruth standing at a crossroads, torn between two worlds, the one she had always known, and the one Naomi was leading her into. She wasn't just choosing between Moab and Bethlehem; she was choosing between the comfort of familiarity and the faith required to step into the unknown. Her words in (***Ruth 1:16*** NLT) still echo with power today: *"Where you go, I will go, and where you stay, I will stay. Your people will be my people, and your God my God."*

That was not a casual statement. It was a declaration of loyalty, faith, and surrender. From Ruth's perspective, this relationship wasn't just about what she could gain; it was about what she could contribute. She wasn't just a recipient—she was a willing participant in the process.

- Ruth contributed honor—she never treated Naomi as a mere in-law, but as a spiritual guide worthy of respect.
- She contributed trust—she followed Naomi's wisdom even when it didn't make sense.

- She contributed commitment—she didn't abandon Naomi in hardship but stayed and labored alongside her.
- She contributed obedience—when Naomi gave instructions regarding Boaz, Ruth didn't argue or resist; she followed in faith.

Ruth's story teaches us that spiritual daughters have a role to play. They are not just receivers of wisdom—they are cultivators of relationships, carriers of honor, and participants in their own growth.

Spiritual mentorship is a two-way street. Just as a mother pour in, a daughter must be willing to receive, apply, and honor the process.

Boundaries and the Role of a Spiritual Mother

Ruth respected Naomi's position in her life.

Naomi understood her role in Ruth's journey.

And because of that mutual understanding, their relationship flourished. Now, imagine if Naomi had overstepped—if she had become overly involved in Ruth's personal life, trying to control her every move. Imagine if Ruth had disregarded Naomi's guidance, treating her words as optional advice instead of divine wisdom. Their story would have looked very different. The reality is spiritual motherhood requires balance. It requires:

✓ **Knowing when to speak and when to be silent.**
✓ **Knowing when to guide and when to let go.**
✓ **Knowing when to correct and when to simply pray.**

There is a difference between being a spiritual mother and being an emotional crutch. As women in ministry, we must walk in wisdom, honoring the boundaries God has set in place.

The Beauty of Spiritual Mentorship

As a woman called to lead, mentor, and mother in the spirit, I have learned this:

- Not every spiritual daughter will stay, but the jewels you impart will remain.
- Not every relationship will be easy, but the lessons will always bear fruit.
- Not every season will feel rewarding, but the investment in someone's future is never wasted.

This journey of spiritual motherhood has been one of the most beautiful, humbling, and stretching assignments of my life.

Conclusion

If you are called to be a spiritual mother, mentor, or leader, embrace the privilege with humility, but never forget the boundaries. If you are walking as a spiritual daughter, value the wisdom, covering, and guidance that God has placed in your life. Because at the end of the day, spiritual motherhood is not about control or authority—it is about stewardship and trust.

And when done right, it produces something beautiful—a legacy of faith, wisdom, and divine purpose.

You Got The Jewels But I Got The Dagger

Journal Your Personal Prayer:

What Readers Are Saying…

Your use of the relationship between Ruth and Naomi as an example of spiritual mentorship was beautiful. It illustrated the depth of these connections and the privilege it is to be invited into a relationship of this caliber. I especially appreciated the emphasis on safety and boundaries in these relationships. Too often, spiritual mentorship lacks structure, leading to unhealthy dynamics. Your insights on presence vs. prayers were also profound—sometimes, what people need most is not just our intercession, but our intentional presence in their lives. Structurally, this chapter was well-organized and easy to follow, with a strong biblical parallel that reinforced your message. I loved how you broke down the essence of spiritual parenting—what truly builds the Kingdom and what does not. Too often, leadership in the church can become about control rather than nurture, and you made a clear distinction between the two. "Spiritual parenting does not demand submission through fear!"

This was a bold and necessary statement "True leadership in the Kingdom is not about coercion but about cultivation." "Don't use your office as a throne but as an altar!"—Powerful! Leadership should always be about service, not status.

Pastor Portia Taylor
Victory Christian Ministries Charles County
Waldorf, MD

Chapter Twelve

Ruth's Perspective
(The Heart of A Spiritual Daughter)

The Heart of a Dedicated Spiritual Daughter

I cannot walk away from this book without talking about the heart of a dedicated spiritual daughter. How can you adequately describe a woman who understands the beauty of daughtership—who embraces the role not as servitude but as an opportunity for lifelong transformation? There is something profoundly powerful about a daughter who walks in humility, honors her spiritual mother, and submits to the process—not out of obligation, but out of revelation. She doesn't lose herself in the role, nor does she see it as mere tradition. Instead, she understands that this relationship is a gift—one that will shape her life for decades to come.

You know, I started this book talking about the daggers, but the truth is, there are spiritual daughter-spiritual mother relationships that are bringing glory to the kingdom. These relationships have tapped into the heart of God, and as a result, they are walking out divine destiny together.

This is how I see Ruth.

One day, she stood at a crossroads, torn between two worlds—the one she had always known, and the one Naomi was leading her into. I can imagine Ruth walking beside Naomi, leaving Moab behind, wondering so many things:

- *What does the future hold?*
- *Am I making the right decision?*
- *Will I regret leaving my past behind?*

But even with all these questions, she chose to walk forward in faith.

- She didn't just leave a place—**she embraced a promise**.
- She didn't just follow Naomi—**she followed purpose**.

And in doing so, Ruth became the perfect example of a spiritual daughter who understands the power of divine alignment. A powerful verse that reflects Ruth's spirit of divine alignment—beyond Ruth 1:16—is **Proverbs 3:5-6 (NIV):** *"Trust in the Lord with all your heart and lean not on your own understanding; in all your ways submit to him, and he will make your paths straight."*

This verse beautifully captures Ruth's posture. She didn't rely on logic, familiarity, or personal comfort—she trusted in the God of Naomi, submitted to His plan, and followed a path that would ultimately position her in divine destiny. Her willingness to align her life with spiritual leadership and God's direction is a living example of what it means to walk by faith, not by sight.

She wasn't just a recipient—she was a willing participant in the process.

- Ruth contributed honor—she never treated Naomi as a mere in-law, but as a spiritual guide worthy of respect.
- She contributed trust—she followed Naomi's wisdom even when it didn't make sense.

- She contributed commitments. She didn't abandon Naomi in hardship but stayed and labored alongside her.

- She contributed obedience—when Naomi gave instructions regarding Boaz, Ruth didn't argue or resist; she followed in faith.

Ruth's story is such a powerful teaching one that teaches the body of Christ a valuable lesson; spiritual daughters have a role to play. They are not just receivers of wisdom—they are cultivators of relationships, carriers of honor, and participants in their own growth.

Spiritual mentorship is a two-way street. Just as a mother pour in, a daughter must be willing to receive, apply, and honor the process.

REAL TALK MOMENT

I can't walk away without speaking on the obvious. I've talked about the beautiful relationships in the body of Christ that are truly bringing glory to the Kingdom—those God-ordained connections that are walking in alignment, honor, and purpose.

But "real talk" there is another reality that must be addressed "there are horror stories too." Many leaders have been **<u>wounded deeply</u>** by those they've poured into. I am one of those leaders.

There have been daughters who once walked closely but allowed jealousy, comparison to creep in, bitterness, gossip and distractions to turn admiration-into-envy and honor-into-division and they stop honoring my god-ordained position in their lives. And that has always been a place of sadness for me. I've shed many tears because of the enemy deceiving my daughters—whispering lies that led them away from the safety of spiritual covering, distorting truth, and causing them to misinterpret love as control and correction as rejection. It's painful to watch them walk into unnecessary battles, knowing they were once under a grace that was designed to protect them.

But as a spiritual mother, I've learned to stay in posture—praying, believing, and trusting that God's hand is still guiding them, even from a distance. Because love doesn't give up when alignment is broken; it waits, covers, and hopes for restoration. And I am fully aware some will return, and others will not, but my prayer doesn't change.

I have heard of many stories where the daughter or son desired the shoes of the parents so badly that instead of walking beside them, they put daggers in their back. And so, I want to lovingly speak to the spiritual children for a moment—**always check your heart**.

Because way before the disconnection happens God always shows the parent what is about to happen.

Ask Elisha and Gehazi?

I know we talked about them earlier in the book, but I want to review another part of the story for the context of this chapter. "Elisha didn't question Gehazi about where he had been because he didn't know, he questioned him because the father was giving Gehazi the opportunity to check his heart posture and repent." **2 Kings 5:20-27 ERV**

Be sure you're not allowing insecurity, ambition, or offense to blind you from the beauty of the covering God placed in your life. A spiritual child's role is not to compete with the parent but to help develop you. And if you're not careful, you'll forfeit the "jewels" because you mishandled the one God sent to give them to you.

….and "the truth will set us free" John 8:32

Conclusion

As daughters in ministry, we must never view our position as one of mere servitude or feel unappreciated in the relationship. We have to see the value of the whole picture. Our role is not just to receive but to contribute—to honor, to support, and to engage in the process of growth with an open and willing heart.

Our presence in the life of a mentor should bring life, not drain it. It should refresh, strengthen, and edify. When the relationship is functioning as God intended, there should be a bond of understanding, love, support, and wisdom—a mutual exchange that fosters both growth and purpose.

Our need to be cultivated, to be bathed in wisdom, should pull our spiritual parents closer to the mouth of God. They should feel the weight of our expectation, not as a burden, but as a sacred responsibility—knowing that their words, prayers, and guidance are shaping the future of the kingdom.

This is why I call my spiritual parents "Purpose Directors." They are not just leaders; they are divine navigators, steering us toward destiny. They seek the wisdom of God on our behalf, not to control us, but to position us for His perfect will.

As daughters, our response must be one of honor, trust, and commitment, just as Ruth exemplified. When we embrace this relationship with the right heart and posture, we will find that the jewels we receive will far outweigh any sacrifice made along the way.

Davronia Val Scarbrough

<u>Journal Your Personal Prayer:</u>

BONUS CHAPTER

Malfeasance

Definition:

Malfeasance in office is any unlawful conduct that is often grounds for a just cause removal of an elected official by statute or recall election.

I cannot allow myself to close this book without addressing something that has left a painful mark on many—*spiritual malfeasance*.

There are people who have stepped into offices they were never called to. They have positioned themselves as spiritual fathers and mothers without the grace, the heart, or the divine appointment to do so. And in turn, they have wounded many, misled many, and even caused some to walk away from the kingdom.

This is not a small issue. This is a reality that many have faced, and some are still healing from.

But let me be clear: *I will not walk away from this subject projecting a victim voice.*

I am not a victim, and the people of God should not be used because they have a heart to serve. We, as leaders, are not victims, nor dictators. We are conquerors and victors, producing winners. That means we do not wallow in what has been done wrong, but we do take responsibility in making sure we operate on what is right.

Spiritual Parenting: What It Is and What It's Not

Spiritual parenting is not about:

- Someone carrying my purse.

- Someone holding my Bible.

- Someone driving me from place to place.

- Someone traveling with me just to say they were in the room.

None of these things define true spiritual parenting. None of these things build the kingdom.

If you, as a spiritual child, have ever encountered behaviors that made you feel *less than*, like you were subservient to someone else's calling, like you were an accessory instead of a *child of God*, I want to say this:

***I apologize for your hurt. I apologize for your mistreatment. I apologize that what was meant to bring you closer to God instead made you question His structure.

There Are Warning Signs

Recognizing the warning signs of spiritual malfeasance is vital for both spiritual leaders and those under their covering. Discerning the signs early, it can prevent deep wounds and long-term damage to faith and trust and most of all to the body of Christ. Here are three warning signs per the bible to be aware of:

1. **Control Disguised as Covenant**
   When a spiritual leader begins to demand blind loyalty, obedience without explanation, or discourages seeking personal revelation from God, this is a red flag. True covenant honors freedom and spiritual growth. **2 Corinthians 3:17 (NIV)** reminds us, *"Where the Spirit of the Lord is, there is freedom."*

2. **Isolation from Accountability**
   If a leader discourages or isolates you from other voices of wisdom, leadership, or your family under the guise of protection or loyalty, it may indicate manipulation. **Proverbs 11:14 (NIV)** says, *"For lack of guidance a nation falls, but victory is won through many advisers."*

3. **Spiritual Gifts Over Character**
   When charisma, gifting, or prophetic accuracy are elevated above integrity, humility, and fruit of the Spirit, you may be witnessing spiritual malfeasance. **Matthew 7:16 (NIV)** says, *"By their fruit you will recognize them."* Gifts may impress, but **fruit confirms true spiritual health.**

But know this—abuse is not the structure of the kingdom, nor is it the heart of God. The spirit of the enemy is abusive. His structure will always bring fruit. His design for spiritual relationships will always bring growth. When spiritual authority is exercised properly, it does not suppress—it cultivates. It does not demand submission through fear—it inspires submission through love.

A Call to Order

We are in a time where God is setting things back in order. The days of people appointing themselves to offices they were never called to will not last. The days of manipulating people under the guise of spiritual authority will not stand. Because when God builds something, it lasts—but when man builds something in his own name, it crumbles.

As an official elected by God to watch over His people, I do not take this calling lightly. And I am speaking to every leader reading this: **do not use your office as a throne, but as an altar.**

An altar is where things are laid down in surrender. A throne is where people seek to be served. If your leadership is built on making others serve you, instead of serving them, you are not walking in true spiritual authority—you are walking in *malfeasance*.

Conclusion: The Kingdom Stands

The kingdom of God is bigger than any one person. It is not built on personalities, titles, or platforms—it is built on Christ. And no matter how many people have been misled, misused, or manipulated, the kingdom will stand. To those who have been hurt (spiritual parent or spiritual son or daughter), I pray this book has helped you heal. I pray it has reminded you that even though man can fail, God never does.

To those who have been called to lead, I pray this book has strengthened you. I pray it has encouraged you to stand firm, to lead well, and to steward the relationships God has placed in your care with honor.

Daggers may come. Misunderstandings may happen. But at the end of it all, **the jewels will remain**. And it is those jewels—the wisdom, the impartation, the lives transformed—that will be the true measure of the legacy we leave behind.

Blessings!

Benediction

Jude 1:24-25 (NKJV)

[24] Now to Him who is able to keep you from stumbling,

And to present you faultless

Before the presence of His glory with exceeding joy

[25] To God our Savior, Who alone is wise,

Be glory and majesty, Dominion and power, Both now and forever.

Amen.

How To Connect

Thank you for taking this journey through *You Got the Jewels, I Got the Dagger.* My prayer is that these words brought healing, perspective, and strength to your walk as a leader, spiritual parent, or son/daughter in the faith.

If this book has blessed your life and you'd like to introduce it to your congregation, ministry team, or mentorship circle, there is a Study Guide available to help deepen the discussion and facilitate growth through guided teaching.

Also, if you would like Pastor Val to come and teach on this subject at your next conference, leadership retreat, or ministry event, she would love to come and share insights, revelation, and tools that bring restoration and clarity to the Body of Christ.

► To Book Pastor Val Visit:

https://www.eddieandvalscarbrough.org/new-page-2

Let's continue to **build the Kingdom together**, with honor, love, and spiritual integrity.

With gratitude,

Pastor Val Scarbrough

#JewelsAndDaggers #SpiritualMentorship #KingdomConnections